# DARING TO DIG

*Mary Anning: Fossil Hunter*

## JANET IVEY-DUENSING

ILLUSTRATED BY KATIE GRAYSON

Traitmarker Books
2984 Del Rio Pike
Franklin, TN 37069

ORDERING BOOKS FOR QUANTITY SALES
Special discounts are available on quantity purchases by corporations, associations, and others. For details, contact the author at the address above.

ATTRIBUTIONS
Interior Text Font: Minion Pro
Interior Title Fonts: Phosphate & Anning
Editors: Sharilyn Grayson
Typesetter: Robbie Grayson III
Cover Design & Interior Illustrations: Katie Grayson

BOOK PUBLISHING INFORMATION
Traitmarker Books
ISBN 978-1-64826-167-1
Published by TRAITMARKER BOOKS
traitmarkerbooks.com
traitmarker@gmail.com

# DARING TO DIG

*Mary Anning: Fossil Hunter*

## JANET IVEY DUENSING

### ILLUSTRATED BY KATIE GRAYSON

# DEDICATED TO

*Mrs. Ernestine Yarborough Jones, Mrs. Dorothy Davidson,*
*Mrs. Rosella Hall, and all the rest of the genius women*
*who have paved the way for me*

*And to Turtledove,*
*Duncan (otherwise known as Optimus Prime),*
*Oona Mae Sunshine, and Magic Felix,*
*I can't wait to see all the genius*
*you will unleash into this world!*

# CONTENTS

Before You Read
Letter to My Genius Self

Letter to Genius You: Author's Note
Other Books to Read
Glossary
Timeline
Other Scientists
About the Author

# Before You Read...

In Mary Anning's lifetime, her knowledge of fossils and her ability to find them helped us understand the nature of our world in a way that had not yet been explored. But Mary Anning's genius still remains unfamiliar to many. In the early 1800s, most geologists and scientists were men. Because of Mary's low standing in society and because she was a woman, she wasn't always given proper credit for her contributions to geology, paleontology, and other branches of science.

For this book, I'm giving Mary the opportunity to tell *her* story and make her genius known. Read this book as if you are opening up a time capsule from Mary Anning, sitting down, and writing a letter to her genius self *and* to the genius in *you!*

At the end of this book, you'll find space to write to your *genius* self and jot down all the amazing things you see yourself doing in the future! It's a bit of a leap of fancy to have this history-making woman write a letter to you cataloging the milestones of her life, but this author thinks that Mary might like knowing that someone gave her an opportunity to tell her own story, make her genius known, and encourage others to DARE TO DIG!

Janet Ivey Duensing | *Nashville, Tennessee*

# LETTER TO GENIUS YOU

Dearest Genius You,

 I am writing this letter not only so that I will remember all that I have accomplished but also so that you and others like you will know a bit about the "girl who loved fossils."

 For anyone who takes the time to know me and read this letter, I just want to tell you to be sure and let your genius shine! Determine to be the best you can be, discover all that you can, and make the world a better place! Let your genius lead you down the path of your purpose and your passion. Most importantly, don't forget to listen. Every discovery has its own sort of sound.

Love
Mary Anning | Lyme Regis, England

# 1
# STROKE OF GENIUS

Dearest Genius You,

This letter might be a bit long, but I want to encourage every bit of your innate magnificence. Here is a recollection and recounting of my life and how I tried to find and follow my genius.

Love,
Mary

When I was a little girl, my passion was looking for treasures on the beach. It was my FAVORITE THING TO DO!

Almost any day of the year, rain or shine, wind or snow, you could find me digging up fossils of fish, plants, and dinosaurs. I am most at home with sand in my shoes and salt water in my hair.

Have you ever heard the tongue twister, *She sells seashells by the seashore?* It goes:

*She sells seashells by the seashore.*
*The shells she sells are surely seashells.*
*So if she sells shells on the seashore,*
*I'm sure she sells seashore shells.*

Well, they say that silly tongue twister was written about me, but I don't think so. I didn't just sell seashells. *I sold fossils!* And I was *a much better finder of fossils* than I was of seashells. I mean, anybody can find a seashell. But can you find a *fossil?*

At the time, tourists to our coastal town called the fossilized items we found *curiosities* or *curios* for short. And to make a sale, my Daddy *never* corrected the tourists. He just called them *curiosities* as well.

We sold *snakestones* (ammonites), *thunderbolts* (belemnites), *devil's toenails* (gryphaea), and *verteberries* (vertebrae).

# DIG THIS!

*Fossils are the remains of plants and animals
whose bones, skeletons, or shells created imprints long ago.*

# SUPER DIG!

*Minerals seep into what is left behind from an animal or plant,
embedding proof of its existence into stone and leaving behind
evidence that the plant or animal was once here.*

# DIG-ALICIOUS!

*The word "fossil" stems from the Latin word "fossillis" which literally
means "dug up." Imagine finding out that digging up fossils is actually
what the word means!*

In Lyme Regis where I was born and have lived all my life, the cliffs and the beaches below them are literally *full* of the remnants of long-ago creatures!

# DIG THIS!

*People thought the coil-shaped, shelled creatures were coiled snakes turned to rock. That's why ammonites were often called "snakestones."*

## SUPER DIG!

*Belemnites were often called "thunderbolts" because people once believed that these fossils rained down from the sky during thunderstorms.*

## SUPER WEIRD DIG!

*"Devil's toenails" were fossilized bivalves related to the living oyster. I mean, they do look like the ugliest toenails I've ever seen!*

But

*I am getting*

# WAAAYYYYY

*ahead of*

*myself!*

I was born on May 21, 1799 in a tiny seaside village called Lyme Regis in the County of Dorset on the southern coast of England. My father was a carpenter who made cabinets and furniture, but he also really loved collecting fossils to sell for extra money to wealthy tourists.

My parents were Richard and Molly Anning. (Mother's name was *Mary,* but everyone called her *Molly).* Maybe when they named me Mary, they thought... *Now things could get a little confusing around here! Ummm. What to do? What to do? How about we call you Mary and your mom Molly?*

# DIG-ALICIOUS!

*Apparently back when every other English girl was named Mary, a common nickname for anyone with that name was Molly. They came to that name simply by replacing the "r" with an "l". What would your nickname be if you replaced one of the letters in your name?*

My parents had 10 children, but only my brother Joseph and I lived into adulthood. I wasn't a very healthy baby. I was ill for the first year or so of my life.

And it is a miracle that I survived childhood. Not only was I a sickly baby, but I was barely more than a year old when I got struck by LIGHTNING! I know! WEIRD, right?

As the story goes, when I was about 15 months old, only a wee toddler, Elizabeth Haskins, my "Aunty Lizzy", came by and offered to take me to the fair. Elizabeth thought that a day outdoors with bright and beautiful things would be good for a listless baby like me.

Horses and riders were performing stunts of all kinds, and the day was full of merry things all around. But at some point during this jolly day, the skies began to darken, and Aunty Lizzy took shelter alongside a couple of other women UNDER A BIG TREE when the storm off the coast blew in.

# DIG THIS!

*Lightning is a sudden electrostatic discharge that occurs typically during a thunderstorm.*

## SUPER DIG!

*Don't stand under a tree during a thunderstorm!*

The rains poured down, the winds blew hard, and the tree and the three ladies and I were all struck by lightning. I was knocked unconscious but still ALIVE! The lightning current surged through my Aunty Lizzie's body. Someone pulled me from her arms and rushed me to my parents and the doctor.

Barely a heartbeat, yet I was still breathing, and they decided to put me in a warm tub of water to revive me. After some time, I finally opened my eyes, wider and brighter and more alive and awake than I had ever been.

Some people around Lyme Regis said I had been such a sickly baby that they didn't have a lot of hope that I would live to be a toddler. AND then I go and get struck by lightning, and all of a sudden, I was unstoppable.

*Almost everyone* who has repeated this part of my story agrees that I became more lively and intelligent and that the lightning made me that way.

27

# DIG THIS!

*Objects struck by lightning experience heat and electro-magnetic forces of great magnitude. Perhaps that lightning strike was my "stroke" of genius.*

I guess I'll never know exactly why my life was spared, but I tried very hard never to waste a minute of my life. I spent it nearly entirely hunting, looking, finding, and learning about fossils.

# 2

# DISSENTERS

Dearest Genius You,

When lightning strikes, I guess that is the right time to get curious! The next time you have one of those "light-bulb" moments, dig deep and find out more about those things that light you up!

Love,
Mary

From that moment on, I was on the move, curious, and going fossil hunting with my Daddy. He taught me how to spot all the best fossils and to see them when other tourists and fossil hunters would pass right by a perfectly good specimen.

Daddy taught me to be curious always, and everything that I know about fossil hunting is because of him.

He even made me my own hammer to use while out hunting for fossils. He taught me how to recognize different kinds of fossils and how to look carefully for them.

He always told my brother and me to be on the lookout for a creature that he believed was lurking somewhere deep in the Blue Lias cliffs of Lyme Regis. I learned a lot of useful things from my dad, from how to unearth a fossil carefully, to how to clean it and make it presentable to sell.

He taught me how to watch for high tides and listen for shifts in rocks and cliffs.

Tourists came to Lyme Regis to fill their curio cabinets with all sorts of curiosities. Thankfully, the sale of the fossils helped keep a roof over our heads and food on our table.

# DIG THIS!

*Around 200 million years ago, the Lyme Regis area lay at the bottom of a Jurassic sea. In my day, fossilized remains of marine animals from the Jurassic Age could be found sticking out from the cliffs and scattered all along the shoreline where I lived.*

# SUPER DIG!

*If you want to go out and try to find a fossil or do some digging, be sure to go slowly and carefully and have a keen eye out for anything that looks interesting.*

While my dad was a carpenter by trade, his carpentry business did not bring in a lot of money, and I grew up very poor. My family attended the Congregationalist Church or the "Church of the Dissenters," a church whose members believed that the people of the congregation, just everyday people, should lead the church.

Perhaps because we didn't go along with what most people believed, Daddy didn't get the carpentry offers he might have. If our beliefs did play a part in our poverty, I'm proud that my parents chose to live and believe what felt right to them, and didn't just go along with the crowd.

Ha! EUREKA! Maybe that's why I had very strong opinions about fossils, science, and the contributions a female can make! Apparently this apple did not fall far from her family tree!

# DIG THIS!

*A Dissenter is someone who doesn't agree with certain opinions or beliefs. In essence, a Dissenter has opposing beliefs, in this instance, opposing religious beliefs. Dissenters believed that their faith could co-exist with the newly emerging discipline of science, and that a stronger belief in God would be the result.*

I learned to read and write in Sunday school. I know that's a weird place to learn your letters and how to read, but I'm telling you the truth.

The Church of the Congregationalists really did believe in the education of the poor … which seems like a thing a church ought to believe in.

# DIG THIS!

*My most prized possession was a bound volume
of the* Dissenters' Theological Magazine and Review, *in which our
family's pastor, the Reverend James Wheaton, had published two
essays, one insisting that God had created the world in six days and
the other urging Dissenters to study the new science of geology.*

# 3

# A Fossil Friendship

Dearest Genius You,

I hope you enjoy reading about science as much as I do! What is your favorite field of scientific study? Do you like plants, animals, oceans, fish, dinosaurs, fossils, biology, or astronomy? There is so much science can teach us! Remember to keep curious always!

Love,
Mary

But one very lucky day, a fancy lady came to the shop and talked to Daddy about all the fossils that we had. She was particularly interested in "fish fossils."

Her name was Elizabeth Philpot. Daddy told her that I was the best fossil finder and would gladly help her find some incredible specimens on the beach. She was a lady of some wealth who thought my ability to find fossils impressive.

So here we go, this fancy lady and me, a wind-scarred girl, showing someone 20 years older where to look for the best fish fossils.

When we got back to the shop on Broad Street, a life-long friendship had been forged. Ms. Elizabeth Philpot even hired my Daddy to make her a cabinet to put all her fossils. She came by often. She gave me my first book on geology.

That book is still on my nightstand, nearly in tatters, but I have read it cover to cover so many times I can't even count.

Elizabeth was my friend and mentor. I'd like to think that I helped her as much as she helped me. I hope and pray that you find a friend as true as Elizabeth was to me. It is a mystery why this lady of some means would befriend us Annings. Maybe she saw more in me than I did at that time.

She and her sisters lived together in Lyme Regis, and while she was well-known for her fish fossil collection, the Philpots also made a soothing salve that they sold to folks. You could use it for chapped hands and faces, scrapes, scratches, stings, cuts, bruises, or just to keep your hands soft.

We couldn't afford it, but whenever she stopped by and asked for my help to hunt fossils, she would always leave a jar for my mother to put on my wind-chapped face and hands. *I smile as I remember that gift.*

My mom had long since lost most of her ability to be soft towards me and my brother. After the loss of eight children, maybe it was hard for her to summon anything tender.

But that healing salve didn't just soothe my chapped face and hands; it soothed a longing in me to have the attention of my mother.

My family lived so close to the sea that the same storms that swept along the cliffs to reveal the fossils sometimes flooded our home. One time the water got so high in the house that we had to crawl out of an upstairs bedroom window to keep from drowning.

Sometimes my mom and dad would argue. My mom wanted my dad to work more as a carpenter, but I believe that Daddy loved hunting for fossils a lot more than he loved building cabinets and doing woodwork.

46

## DIG THIS!

*Fossils can be found by digging with a shovel or pick, and sometimes an earthquake or a volcano reveals them. Usually, I discovered my fossil finds after the wind and water wore away the layers of earth and rock that had encased them millions of years ago in what is now called the Jurassic Coast.*

# 4
# HARD TIMES

Dearest Genius You,

Has there ever been a time when your family didn't have enough money for all the bills? Have you ever gone hungry? Ever had no heat? I'm so sorry, because I have had all these things be my reality. Sometimes, life requires you to get really creative so that things get better, I believe in you!

Love,
Mary

In 1807 we really needed money, so Daddy decided not to wait until the tourists made it all the way to Lyme Regis and down the hill to Broad Street to buy a fossil.

He went to meet them and get a jump start on potential sales by taking his fossils directly to them as they arrived at Charmouth for their seaside holiday.

One night coming home from Charmouth, my dad slipped and fell from a cliff called the Black Ven, known for frequent rock slides. The fog had been thick, and he lost his footing and fell down the steep cliff. He already had tuberculosis, and the fall was the beginning of the end for my dad. He could no longer work or go fossil hunting with us. THAT was something I thought I'd never see.

I quit going to school that year. I WAS JUST EIGHT YEARS OLD, and I never attended regular school again. I don't advise this. However, in the early 1800s, this is what I had to do to help my family make money. After the fall, Daddy was too sick to work. My mom was a seamstress. She tried her best to earn money by sewing for others.

When my Daddy died in 1810, things got tough, and I mean TOUGH! He died owing a lot of money, and we had to work extra hard to keep ourselves from being out on the streets without a home.

I went out to the shore and the cliffs every day to look for fossils. I tell you this truly: not a day goes by that I don't miss my Daddy and wish a thousand times for just another day of digging with him.

Sometimes I can still hear him whisper, *Keep a keen eye, my girl!*

For several years after Daddy died, we received a little money and food and a few clothes from the Overseers of the Poor. We weren't the only ones to need help. This was an especially hungry time for many in England. Food had become extraordinarily expensive due to the wars Napoleon Bonaparte fought to conquer Europe.

# DIG THIS!

*Napoleon Bonaparte was the Emperor of France
and Military Commander of the Napoleonic Wars 1803-1815.*

Thankfully, one day I found a most perfect ammonite, a coiled fossil with not one blemish, and while I was admiring my find, I walked smack dab into a lady on the beach.

She wanted to see what I had in my hand, and the minute she laid eyes on the perfectly intact ammonite, she offered me a half crown for the beauty!

# DIG THIS!

*The half crown was a British coin worth two shillings and sixpence, or one-eighth of a pound. It was equal to about 60 cents in U.S. money at that time. The half crown was first issued in 1549, in the reign of Edward VI.*

# SUPER DIG!

*The half crown (2 shillings, 6 pence) would equal nearly $50.00 by today's standards.*

It's hard to imagine that 60 cents could help buy food for a whole week, but I assure you: it is true!

Why did the fancy lady want the perfect ammonite I found? Well, people really loved ammonites and thought they were good luck charms that would help keep snakes and EVIL away. Maybe the good lady believed these things, too!

But to tell you the truth, it really didn't matter to me why the lady wanted the beautiful ammo I had found! I ran home and gave the half crown instantly to my mother! Talk about a proud moment for me!

My mom might not have liked fossils so much, but she certainly didn't mind them when they brought in money to help us pay the rent and buy food!

From that day forward, I knew that my job was to go out to the beach and comb the cliffs for fossils.

This was a HUGE moment in my life. I knew what I was good at doing, and I knew that because of this talent my Daddy had passed down to me, somehow finding fossils was my purpose in life.

Writing that down just now makes me believe that maybe ammonites are indeed good luck charms!

# DIG THIS!

Ammonites were aquatic animals that were protected by a spiral coiled shell made from calcium.

# SUPER DIG!

The ammonite lived in the outer largest chamber of the many chambers in its shell. Ammonites went extinct about 65 million years ago, but they may be the ancestors of the squid and the octopus.

# DIG-ALICIOUS!

What's your good luck charm? What is something you think brings you good luck?

# 5

# MONSTER IN THE CLIFFS

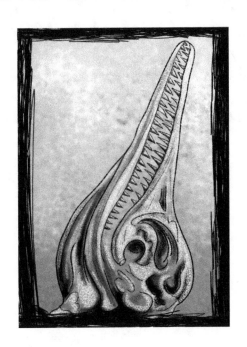

Dearest Genius You,

I now consider you a real friend. Thank you for continuing to read my letter to you. I hope you are beginning to think about what you are good at doing!

Love,
Mary

Another moment that would change everything happened in 1811, when my brother Joseph found the biggest fossil we had ever uncovered. It was a skull, a long one, nearly 4 feet LONG with a pointy snout and lots and lots of sharp teeth.

UGHHHH! I still get a little jealous thinking he's the one that found the head of the creature!

My dad had always told us tall tales about a great creature hidden in the cliffs of Lyme Regis, and Joseph had found the head of the thing! It was exciting, but it's hard to tell somebody what you found when you DON'T KNOW what exactly you've found.

Was it a crocodile, an alligator, or a porpoise? AND WHERE WAS THE REST OF IT? And how on earth would I ever, ever be able to get it out of this cliff?

Joseph helped, of course, and he deserves the credit for being the fossil hunter who found the head of the beast! But he needed to make money to support Mama and me; so the rest of the finding of this humongous fossil now was firmly my responsibility! Can you imagine a young girl in a hat and petticoats, out there barking orders at grown men about how to be careful not to hurt the fossil or break this long-ago creature in any way?

It took me months to dig it all the way out and put it all together properly. I'd like to say a special thank you to the nice fellas who helped me unearth it. I couldn't have done it without them. I mean, I was only 12!

You can only imagine the crazy names I got called. Some people called me a "miracle child" because I survived the lightning strike. Others called me "evil" and "a friend of the devil," because how else could I have survived that firebolt from the skies unless I had made a deal with the dark side? I personally liked being called MIRACLE CHILD!

I didn't always like the names I got called, but I decided it made little difference to me. I let it roll off my back like salt water. Remember: when people are mean or unkind, call you names, bully you, or make fun of you FOR ANY REASON ... what they do says WAAYYY more about THEM than it ever does about YOU. You just keep on being you, just like I kept on digging that creature out of the cliff!

Most people thought we had just found a big ole CROCODILE! But it didn't look like any of the crocodiles folks already knew about. SO WHAT WAS IT?

After I had assembled the entire skeleton of the creature carefully together, a gentleman named Lord Henry Hoste Henley of Colway Manor bought it for 23 pounds, which would have been about $110.60 in U.S. currency at the time. But for us Annings, it seemed like a million dollars!

## DIG THIS!

*All assembled, this ancient sea creature, when reunited with its 4 foot skull, measured an amazing 17 feet long. YIKES! That's nearly the height of 3 tall men!*

## SUPER DIG!

*According to an historical conversion of currency, £23 would be more than £1,600 or $2,000 in today's money—enough to purchase six months of food for the Anning family.*

## DIG-ALICIOUS!

*Can you believe that my brother Joseph was just 15 years old and I was just 12 when we discovered a skull and the entire skeleton of an ancient sea creature?*

After that sale, my mom stopped being so grumpy about me always looking for fossils and started helping me sell them and making sure we got paid for all my fossil finds.

# BUT GET THIS!

Lord Henry Hoste Henley turned around and sold my fossil to William Bullock's Museum of Natural Curiosities in London. Because he owned the land on which the fossil had been found, his name appeared as the person who had unearthed it! HOW UNFAIR IS THAT?

Adding injury to insult, William Bullock dressed this ancient, scientific treasure in a vest and placed a monocle over its eye. A sign pinned to the vest read "Crocodile in a Fossil State." My amazing find was nothing more than a JOKE IN A SILLY COSTUME!

All those months of hard work! I can't even tell you how my heart hurt when Ms. Philpot told me the news. She and her sisters had gone to London to visit their brother and wanted to see what had become of our creature. Let me just tell you that making a discovery only to have it made a mockery of will really ANNOY a girl! Yet, there was nothing to do but keep on digging for my next great find!

It was during this time that Henry De La Beche moved to Lyme Regis. Henry could draw ANYTHING! He followed me around ALL THE TIME asking me all kinds of questions, and I taught him how to find fossils and see what others missed. He is my forever friend who holds a very special place in my heart. While he was from some wealth and high society, Henry spent a lot of time with Joseph and me on the beach. I taught him all that I knew about fossils and rocks.

He likes to tell folks that his great love for geology happened because of his friendship with me. And I like to say his deep and abiding friendship meant more to me over the years than any fossil I ever found.

In 1814, Everard Home published a scientific paper on the skeleton. Everard, EVER-WHATEVER, actually published a series of six papers on the creature ALL THE WHILE DESCRIBING IT AS A CROCODILE!

UGHHH! It's not a crocodile! It is SOMETHING OTHER! And did I mention that Mr. Fancy Pants Home DID NOT give Joseph or me even a mention, much less credit, for what we found?

Finally in 1819, the fossil was sold to the British Museum of Natural History, where Charles Konig removed the ridiculous get up and finally gave it its proper name: ICHTHYOSAUR!

# DIG THIS!

*Ichthyosaur means fish lizard. The word combines two Greek words: Ιχθυς or Ichthys meaning "fish" and σαυρος or sauros meaning "lizard." They are large, extinct marine reptiles.*

# SUPER DIG!

*In time it would be discovered that an ichthyosaur was an extinct reptile (from the Mesozoic era) resembling a dolphin, with a long pointed head, four flippers, and a vertical tail.*

# DIG-ALICIOUS!

*The Mesozoic Era is an interval of geological time from 252 to about 66 million years ago. It is also called the Age of Reptiles!*

But Joseph didn't get credit for the find at that time, and I didn't get credit for the find, not for a while at least … which kind of makes me just a little bit mad. I mean, I was very proud of myself knowing what we had done and the fact that I was only a girl!

I'm just grateful people stopped calling it a crocodile once it had its proper name: ICHTHYOSAUR! THANK GOODNESS!

# DIG THIS!

*What Joseph and I had uncovered was the most complete example of an ichthyosaur anyone had ever found EVER! And no matter who gets the credit, that is something that cannot be taken away from us.*

# 6

# A PALEONTOLOGIST

Dearest Genius You,

What do you think? What can you do no matter your age? What can you create or discover?

Love,
Mary

The more fossils I found, the more and more I wanted to know, and since I needed to hunt for fossils to help my family, I tried to learn as much as possible. I was always reading something about geology and fossils. If it mentioned fossils… you can bet I read it. Ms. Philpot shared any books or scientific journals she happened to come across with me. WHAT A GIFT IT IS TO READ and LEARN!

Do you love to read and learn about something you are very curious about?

But even with all my smarts about fossils, my family found it hard to keep food on the table. One time my mom sold all our furniture just to keep us under one roof. Sleeping on the floor IS NOT the same as sleeping in a bed, I gotta tell you.

That's about the time that my brother Joseph had an opportunity to learn how to upholster furniture. "Upholster" is just a big, weird word that means putting fabric or leather on furniture. He would continue to help hunt for fossils when he wasn't working as an apprentice in the upholstery shop; however, Joseph needed to get skilled at something that would provide a good week's wage. That is also about the time when it comes in handy to have good friends. Lieutenant Thomas Birch was one such friend. Over the years, he had purchased a lot of fossils from us.

# DIG THIS!

*My family had sold our furniture to pay the rent. Lieutenant Birch was concerned for our family and decided to do something to help. He hed an auction in London of all the fossils he had purchasd from us in Lyme Regis.*

He wrote to a fellow fossil hunter, Gideon Mantell, on March 5th of that year to say that the sale was "for the benefit of the poor woman and her son and daughter at Lyme, who have in truth found almost ALL the fine things which have been submitted to scientific investigation … I may never again possess what I am about to part with, yet in doing it I shall have the satisfaction of knowing that the money will be well applied."

# DIG THIS!

*Gideon Mantell, a doctor whose passion was looking for fossils and inspired by Mary Anning's discoveries, began to catalog fossils and plants found near his home in Sussex, England.*

I'll never exactly know why Thomas Birch did such a kind thing, but I will always be grateful for his generosity and show of support. What he did by having the charity auction for us provided some much-needed financial stability for my family.

It makes me believe that in some small way, a wealthy, fossil-collecting gentleman of the highest order and of an entirely different class than me was saying that my work was important… and that, I believe, is the greatest gift Lieutenant Birch could have ever given me.

Because of this great gift, my work continued. Cold and often alone, out I went, which I rather liked a lot. I would dig and unearth the most precious of treasures. When you are poor and your petticoats look like you have rolled in the mud, well, people steer clear. All except for Ms. Elizabeth Philpot.

Ms. Philpot had quite the fish fossil collection. She was super knowledgeable about fossil fish and had assembled a large array of specimens. Even though there was a 20-year difference in our ages, I think when we were out looking for fossils on the beach, she was a just a girl like me, enjoying digging in the sand!

In truth, Elizabeth was one of my dearest friends. For us hunting fossils was like looking to put together some yet unseen puzzle … and I know for me, I was determined to find all the pieces I could.

# DIG THIS!

*Elizabeth Philpot was an early 19th-century British fossil collector, amateur paleontologist, and artist who collected fossils from the cliffs around Lyme Regis.*

Ms. Philpot often found herself in the company of leading geologists and paleontologists of our time, including William Buckland and Louis Agassiz, both of whom she was generous enough to introduce to me.

I can never repay her for all that she did to make sure my fossil finds got into the right hands and that all the learned folks knew about what I was doing.

I should also like to take a moment to thank my mother, Molly Anning. She wasn't the most attentive nor the tenderest, but in 1821, she wrote a letter to the British Museum requesting (some might say demanding) payment for a specimen which they had gotten from our Anning's Fossil Depot. They responded not long after, with a PAYMENT! My mother wasn't going to let anyone take credit for a specimen THEY DIDN'T FIND, without at LEAST paying for it. WAY TO GO, MUM!

In 1821, my fossil finding was stupendous! I found three fossilized ichthyosaur skeletons, ranging from 5 to 20 feet long. In that same year, my dear friend Henry de la Beche and William Conybeare co-wrote a paper describing the ichthyosaurs that several other fossil hunters and I had found.

# DIG THIS!

*In 1821, Henry De La Beche and William Conybeare co-wrote a paper for the Geological Society that contained an important description and analysis of all that had been learned to that point about the anatomy of ichthyosaurs, including the fact that there had been at least three different species.*

One of the fossilized ichthyosaur skeletons I discovered was like nothing I'd ever seen before. As soon as I saw the skull of the thing, I literally jumped back. Its eye sockets were SUPER HUGE, and the long-ago creature seemed to be staring at me!

HAHA! Maybe that was its way of getting my attention and making sure it was discovered!

However, this was a very different kind of ichthyosaur. This one would be called the TEMNODONTOSAURUS PLATYODON!

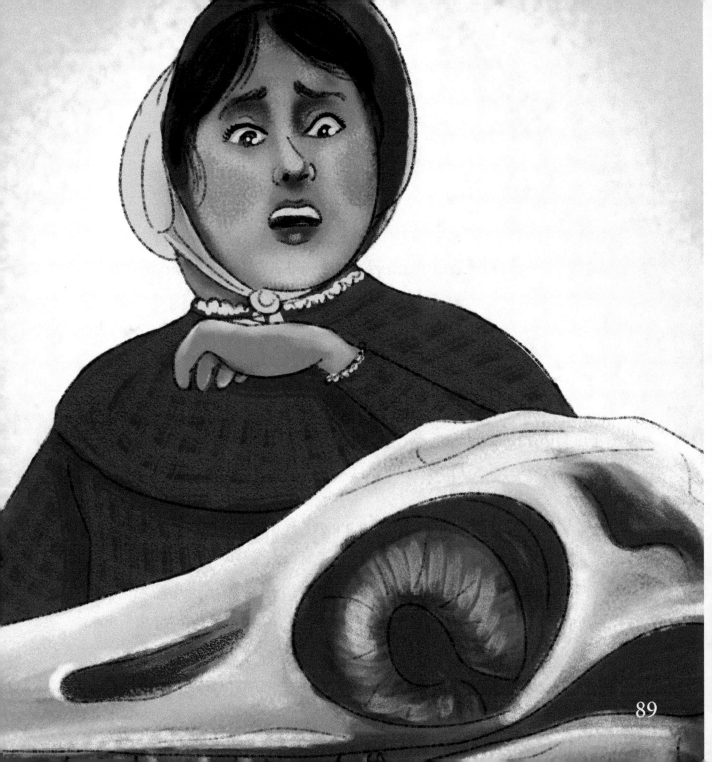

# DIG THIS!

*The eyes of ichthyosaurs are very LARGE in comparison to the size of the body.*

## SUPER DIG!

*Ichthyosaurs hold the record for eye size: the largest ever recorded for any known vertebrate was 10.4 inches/264mm in diameter from the species TEMNODOTOSAURUS PLATYODON!*

## DIG-ALICIOUS!

*Vertebrates are a large group of animals distinguished by the possession of a backbone or spinal column, including mammals, birds, reptiles, amphibians, and fishes.*

Many learned people came to our Fossil Depot to talk to me about what I knew and had found lurking in the cliffs and sandy seabed around Lyme Regis.

People would come by just to watch me take great care to clean and remove dirt and debris from my fossils. It was a lot of work to find them; so I most certainly wasn't going to mess one up by being careless.

Sometimes I would make a frame and glue a fossil together piece by piece. I kept reading and studying my science books, and I drew pictures of everything that I found. I had read enough to know that the most learned geologists were METICULOUS, meaning very careful and slow, to make sure they took good care of their data or specimen.

In 1822, Henri Marie Ducrotay de Blanville, editor of *Journal de Physique*, coined the word "paleontology" to refer to the study of ancient living organisms through fossils. As discoveries of prehistoric life continued to emerge, more and more was understood about the history and age of the Earth.

Can you believe it? I was a paleontologist BEFORE THE WORD EVER EVEN EXISTED!

# DIG THIS!

*Paleontology, also spelled* palaeontology, *is the scientific study of life of the geologic past that involves the keen analysis of plant and animal fossils preserved in rocks.*

# SUPER DIG!

*Paleontology is concerned with all aspects of the biology of ancient life forms.*

# DIG-ALICIOUS!

*The term itself originates from Greek παλαιός, palaios, "old, ancient", ὄν, on (from ontos), "being, creature," and λόγος, logos, "speech, thought, or study." So PALEONTOLOGY is the study of old creatures!*

# 7
# NOT A FAKE

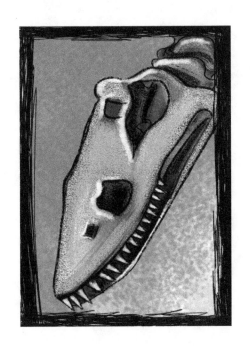

Dearest Genius You,

Has the word for what your genius will discover even been invented yet? Just think... you could be the first of something altogether yet unknown.

Love,
Mary

M uch to my delight and SURPRISE, George Cumberland mentioned me in an article in the *Bristol Mirror* in 1823! He wrote, "This persevering female has for years gone daily in search of fossil remains of importance at every tide, for many miles under the hanging cliffs at Lyme, whose fallen masses are her immediate object, as they alone contain these valuable relics of a former world, which must be snatched at the moment of their fall, at the continual risk of being crushed by the half suspended fragments they leave behind, or be left to be destroyed by the returning tide– to her exertions we owe nearly all the fine specimens of Ichthyosauri of the great collections."

I have to tell you that I grinned from ear to ear as I read that! WOW! To think that those words had been written about me! Not too shabby for a self-taught girl like me!

# DIG THIS!

*Guess what? I'm an autodidact! That's a person who has learned a subject without the benefit of a teacher or formal education, a self-taught person.*

## SUPER DIG!

*Are you an autodidact? If not, what subject might you want to learn all on your own? What subject would most interest you to learn all by yourself?*

On December 10, 1823, I made one of the most important discoveries of my lifetime. While scanning the beach near the very cliff that was responsible for the ultimate demise of my Daddy, I came upon a skull that was unlike anything I'd ever seen before. The majority of the skulls I'd found belonged to ichthyosaurs; they were long and narrow, a bit like the heads of dolphins or crocodiles. This skull, on the other hand, was small, beady-eyed, and had a mouthful of strange, needle-shaped teeth.

Again, I cannot say thank you enough to the local fellas who were willing to help me get the creature free from its place in the Blue Lias cliff. With their help, I unearthed the rest of this mysterious specimen, which looked even WEIRDER than the skull of the bizarre thing!

Attached to a wide torso and broad pelvis were four flippers and a pint-sized tail. It had a snake-like neck, the head of a lizard, crazy crocodile-like teeth, weird ribs, and the paddles or fins of a whale.

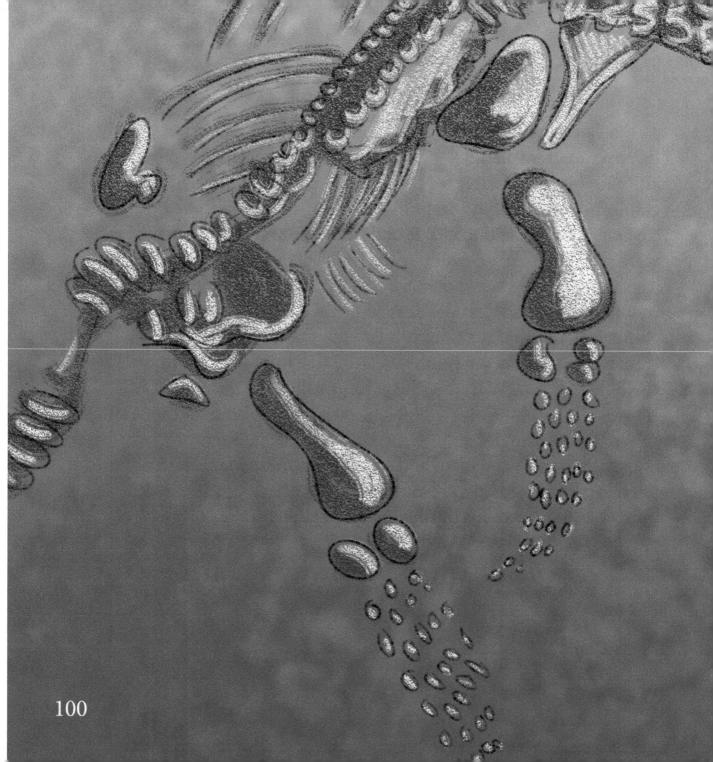

But the TRULY PECULIAR thing about this long-ago sea creature was its SUPER long neck, that made up nearly half of its 9-foot length.

After putting this monster together bone by bone, exactly as I had found it, I contacted the only person that I thought would appreciate my find, paleontologist Reverend William Buckland.

Over the years, I had held some spirited conversations with Reverend Dr. William Buckland about the new kind of science called paleontology.

I have to say: he did not always like my opinions. I mean, I was only 24, but I could hold my own with any geologist or paleontologist. I was that confident in my skills, and it didn't bother me one whit how much learning they had and how very little formal learning I had.

The reason I was so sure of my science was that, as I've mentioned before, there wasn't a single shred of fossil-related news published in scientific journals that I did not read.

## DIG THIS!

*I even taught myself FRENCH so that I could read science
articles published in that language.*

## SUPER DIG!

*This is how I knew that some paleontologists—
including Reverend Dr. Buckland and Reverend William
Conybeare—believed that a few fossil bones previously attributed to
ichthyosaurus really belonged to an as-yet-unidentified
kind of marine reptile.*

Reverend William Conybeare had even figured out a name for this new long ago creature: plesiosaurus.

In my letter to Reverend Dr. Buckland, I sent a very detailed sketch of my newest find. I was even so bold to write to him, "I may venture to assure you that it is the only [plesiosaurus skeleton] discovered in Europe."

Ha ha! What do you think of that? I wasn't even an educated woman or really allowed to be one, yet here I was telling a very well-known and respected GEOLOGIST that I had indeed found the first plesiosaurus EVER! And I don't say that in any kind of boastful way. I just knew that I had found what they had been hypothesizing! And I wasn't just guessing; I had put it together bone by bone. So I knew that it was something that no one had ever found before…the first ever completely intact plesiosaur.

# DIG THIS!

*Plesiosaurus comes from the Greek words,*
*πλησιος, plesios, "near to", and σαυρος, sauros, "lizard". In other,*
*more simple words, it is near to a lizard.*

# SUPER DIG!

*Plesiosaurus was a plesiosaur, a type of marine reptile. It was not a*
*dinosaur, though it coexisted with many dinosaurs.*

# DIG-ALICIOUS!

*Most people agreed that a plesiosaur looked like a snake threaded*
*through the shell of a turtle. Prior to my find and detailed sketch,*
*nobody had any idea about what this mysterious animal looked like.*

Once he finished reading my description, Buckland talked Richard Grenville, the first Duke of Buckingham, into buying the fossilized skeleton.

The animal's proportions were so bizarre that some scientists cried "FOUL." There were even scientists who believed I had FAKED the plesiosaur and had used any old bone I had lying around to glue it all together.

Upon seeing a copy of my sketch, the legendary French anatomist Baron Georges Cuvier said that the fossil I had found and put together was a hoax, a farce, and an utter exaggeration of fact!

In a letter to Conybeare, Cuvier asked, "How could an animal with such an absurdly long neck possibly exist?" Cuvier said basically, "I don't believe this creature ever existed."

George Cuvier basically accused me of putting various pieces of fossils together all willy-nilly out of some crazy delusion that I was actually a real fossilist.

He even went further to suggest that I had attached a snake's skull and vertebrae to the body of an ichthyosaurus.

Well, WELL, Mr. Cuvier! It is I who shall have the last word. It took a bit of stamping my feet and saying LOUDLY … NO! I FOUND EVERY PIECE, NUMBERED EACH ONE, AND THIS IS EXACTLY THE CREATURE I FOUND! Thank you very much!

In due time, it became clear by my very detailed drawings and sketches that I had in no way tampered with the specimen that I had found!

After an up-close and personal examination of the fossilized creature, the famous naturalist and geologist was forced to eat his words and admit that I indeed had found a plesiosaur!

## DIG THIS!

*Do you ever draw your science? Give it a try. It might help you understand science concepts more clearly.*

## SUPER DIG!

*After much research, scientists discovered that a plesiosaur used all four flippers to power through the water. The biggest thrust doesn't come from the front or rear flippers alone, but through a harmonious combination of both.*

# 8

# PRINCESS OF PALEONTOLOGY

Dearest Genius You,

Has anyone ever doubted or made fun of something that you drew or put together? Remember this. Never, never give up on your science!

Love,
Mary

At an 1824 Geological Society of London meeting, Conybeare presented a very well-received lecture on the near-perfect specimen of a plesiosaurus from Lyme Regis. Reverend William Conybeare also published a paper on the plesiosaur I had unearthed featuring my detailed original illustrations. He mentioned me neither in his presentation nor in his scientific paper.

Conybeare was just one among many geologists who furthered their own careers by writing papers about fossils that I HAD FOUND!

These gentleman, and I mean that not in the most flattering way, rarely if EVER gave credit where credit was due, namely to me! And to make matters more confounding, I couldn't publish my own findings in fancy-schmancy science journals, BECAUSE the editors of those publications didn't accept submissions from women.

UGHHHHHH!!!!!! One day I hope this kind of prejudiced thinking will end! Just because I am female does NOT mean I don't have smart things to say.

# DIG THIS!

*After making such a fuss that I had somehow falsified the fossil of the plesiosaur, George Cuvier wrote in 1824 that my plesiosaur was "the most amazing creature ever discovered." Well, at least that is SOMETHING!*

On several different occasions over the years, I told my friend Maria Pinney that the world had used me ill and that I DID NOT like it one bit!

Learned men devoured my brains and made a great deal by publishing works whose contents I furnished, while I got none of the advantages.

And once when an admirer of my work wrote a letter to me, I actually sent back a rather offending letter that said, "I beg your pardon for distrusting your friendship. The world has used me so unkindly, I fear it has made me suspicious of everyone."

Yet while I was denied the recognition that I felt I both desired and deserved, do you know what I did?

I just kept right on digging and discovering! I wasn't going to let anything stop me from fossil hunting! In 1824, Lady Harriet Silvester came to my Anning Fossil Shop. She later said of me that it was extraordinary that I had taught myself so much about the science of fossils that the moment I found any fossilized bones, I knew just what species they belonged to.

She even went on to say that some of the cleverest men agree that I understood fossils better than anyone else in the kingdom.

That was truly high praise from someone so high society!

Some people actually called me the "Princess of Paleontology," "Slayer of Dragons," and a "Geological Lioness."

A few dear friends, like William Buckland, George Cumberland, Henry De La Beche, and Charles Lyell, whose students included Charles Darwin himself, believed that what I found had forever changed the way people thought about the world.

You see, up until that time people believed that the world was just 6,000 years old. It was a conundrum like no other. The concept of extinction was a controversial idea, and not widely accepted. Most everyone believed that God's creatures did not die out. The idea of extinction simply didn't exist. But how else could there be stony skeletons of creatures who no longer roamed the earth within heavy layers of rock?

# DIG THIS!

*My fossil discoveries helped lay the foundation of modern thinking and helped us understand the long-ago creatures of our world.*

# 9

# DURIA ANTIQUIOR

Dearest Genius You,

Whatever you can think, create, or imagine today just might be great science tomorrow. Go explore, discover, and dig deeper!

Love,
Mary

By 1825, Joseph had finished his apprenticeship in upholstery, leaving the fossil finding to me and going full-time into the upholstery business. And I managed the fossil finding business quite well, I would like to say!

In 1826, I had earned enough money from fossil sales to move my family to a cottage on upper Broad Street. The main room on the ground level became our new store, complete with an attractive storefront window. It quickly emerged as a major tourist attraction, particularly for geology buffs.

The Annings Fossil Depot hosted geological celebrities like Gideon Mantell, who in 1825 announced the discovery of iguanodon, the first herbivorous dinosaur known to science.

# DIG THIS!

*Herbivorous means feeding on plants!*

Around this time, I also discovered belemnite fossils that contained ink sacs. Upon further investigation, my friend, Ms. Elizabeth Philpot, found that the fossilized ink mixed with water could be used for drawing and painting.

Lucky me! I love to draw my fossil finds; so just imagine: I now could literally draw my fossils with fossil ink! THIS IS WHY I LOVE SCIENCE!

# DIG THIS!

*Pterodactyl means WINGED REPTILE!*

# SUPER DIG!

*Belemnoidea / Belemnites were 10-armed creatures that could eject ink into the water, similar to modern squid or cuttlefish.*

# DIG-ALICIOUS!

*Artists in the town and I began using Belemnoidea ink to draw pictures of fossils found in the area.*

And I just kept on finding fossils! In 1828 I found a pterosaurus, also called a pterosaur, and it was the first time one had ever been found anywhere other than Germany! It was later called a pterodactyl.

Boy, oh boy, did this shake things up! Can you imagine a flying dinosaur? I wish I could have seen one when it was living!

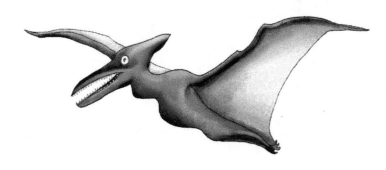

# DIG THIS!

*My find was the first ever discovery of the dimorphodon genus. The species I discovered was Dimorphodon macronyx, to be exact!*

Then, a year later I found the squaloraja, an animal that links sting rays and sharks. And they are definitely related; just take a look! I like to consider them fish cousins. In a way you can think of a sting ray as a flattened shark!

And maybe one of the weirdest things I ever discovered were these fossilized clumps inside the bellies of the ichthyosaurs I had found. I broke one open, and lo and behold, I identified fossilized fish bones and scales. My friend William Buckland came to believe that these "bezoar stones" or clumps of undigested food, were in fact fossilized poop! Yep, you read that right: fossilized poop! I'M NOT EVEN KIDDING!

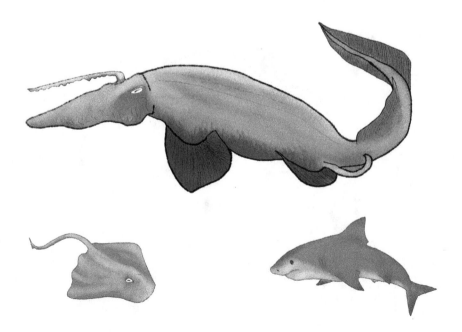

William named them coprolites, meaning dung stones, and while that sounds a bit gross, in a way it was like looking at a time capsule of what these ichthyosaurs had for breakfast, lunch, and dinner!

Trust me when I tell you that I DID NOT set out to find this . . . but that's what being a paleontologist is all about ... you just never know WHAT you are going to discover.

# DIG THIS!

*A Bezoar stone is simply undigested material found in the stomach. It was once believed that bezoar stones had healing magic in them.*

## SUPER DIG!

*People thought that bezoar stones could counteract any poison. They were commonly worn as charms or ground into medicinal powders. GROSS! Who wants to wear a poop necklace? Or drink fossilized dung tea?*

# DIG-ALICIOUS!

*Queen Elizabeth I had a bezoar stone set in a silver ring. YIKES!*

Have I told you how much I love learning about fossils? Maybe one of the best finds that I ever unearthed was when I found an even better, more complete plesiosaur. It truly was one of the most beautiful and complete fossilized creatures I had ever come across. Its official name became … Plesiosaurus macrocephalus.

## DIG THIS!

*A cast of this fossil is on display at the Natural History Museum in Paris, France. You can go see it if you are ever in Paris!*

## SUPER DIG!

*I was paid 45 pounds for that plesiosaur, the equivalent of $200!*

In 1830, my sweet, amazing friend Henry De La Beche painted something he called *Duria Antiquior,* meaning *An Earlier Dorset,* to raise money for me and my family.

His painting was bursting with all the creatures that I had found (he even included reptile dung!). He painted his vision of a prehistoric world. He asked George Sharf to make a lithograph of his painting, and the money from every copy sold was given to me and my family.

In a way, Henry's painting allowed folks to picture what life looked like millions of years ago and consider what processes had occurred that made life look so different in the present.

What a blessed thing it is to have someone like Henry in my life! I'm so glad to call him my friend. Henry used his art to understand his science and his science to understand his art.

# 10
# TRAY AND THE TOP HAT

Dearest Genius You,

Do you have a friend like Henry who believes in you? I sure hope so. Life is so much sweeter with a good friend.

Love,
Mary

Even though we did get paid for the fossils I found, the money coming in was never quite consistent enough to keep all the bills paid.

The years went by, and my great love, other than fossils, was my sweet dog Tray. If I went hunting fossils, so did he. He would carry my pail of tools or sit and guard a new find, making sure mean ole Captain William Lock, or Captain Cury as most folks called him, didn't try and steal what I had just uncovered. Lazy Captain Cury dug fossils with a spade, and he didn't mind if he broke the very fossil he found. Captain Cury didn't have patience or respect for the science he was digging up. He was just interested in making as much money as possible.

Captain Cury loved to follow me and take a fossil as soon as I laid eyes on it. I learned over the years how to avoid him as much as possible.

Tray was very good at making sure Captain Cury didn't come near anything I found, especially when it was too big for me to put in my pail, or if I needed to go get someone to help me carry it back to my Fossil Depot.

Tray went everywhere I went, and quite often I did a lot of fossil hunting after big storms, because the wind and rain created the perfect conditions for the cliffs to reveal something down deep within, which helped me to find some of the very best fossils. It also meant that the cliffs were sometimes SUPER SHIFTY.

One day a cliff gave way, and the rocks and sand and sludge traveled too fast for sweet, faithful Tray to outrun the avalanche of falling debris. I lost my best fur friend that day. I was very lucky the landslide hadn't overtaken me. Over the years, I had many narrow escapes from harm, and this was yet another. Perhaps, as with the lightning, I was a Miracle Child indeed!

141

I wrote to my friend that it must sound silly to be so sad over losing Tray. But he had become my constant companion. I do believe that something shifted that day, not just in the cliffs of Lyme Regis, but something in me.

Digging from then on became a bit slower and sadder. I took to wearing a top hat to protect myself from falling rocks.

You might think, "How could a TOP HAT keep a falling rock from hurting me?" But that was all I had.

Henry drew a cartoon of me in 1833, showing me searching among the cliffs for my next great find.

He wrote a caption for the cartoon that read, "An artist's representation of his dear friend the fossil hunter."

Oh, Henry! What a funny, brilliant fellow you are! But why must you draw me wearing that RIDICULOUS HAT? I might have been a good fossilist and geologist, but that may not have been the best scientific thinking I ever exhibited.

I suppose if you are passionate about something, nothing should stop you from doing what you love… even if it means that sometimes rocks fall and cliffs give way.

So out I went, knee deep in the tides, searching for fossils, alone with my tools and the hammer my Daddy made for me.

# 11
# DARE TO DIG

Dearest Genius You,

Do you have a fur friend that you love very much? My dog Tray was the best. Whether it's a dog or cat or some other animal, it's special to know the love of a fur friend. Fur babies are the best!

Love,
Mary

In 1834, Ms. Philpot and I helped Swiss paleontologist Louis Agassiz study fossil fish. We showed him how to match the backbones and teeth of the fish found in the same layer of limestone. For years, learned men and people of high society would come and visit me and ask for my help in understanding the study of fossils. In a way, we were taking a walk through time as the layers of the cliffs of Lyme Regis gave way and revealed their mysterious treasures.

# DIG THIS!

*The word scientist appeared for the first time in 1834 in William Whewell's review of Mary Somerville's book,* **On the Connexion of Physical Sciences.** *He called Somerville a scientist, in part because "man of science" seemed a tad bit weird and inappropriate when referring to a woman. Whewell wanted a word that "actively celebrated the peculiar illumination of the female mind." To him, she was no mere astronomer, physicist, or chemist, but a visionary thinker who could cross-connect and organize multiple areas of science into one whole picture; thus she must be called A SCIENTIST!*

## SUPER DIG!

*THE FIRST PERSON EVER CALLED A SCIENTIST WAS A FEMALE! GO, GO, GIRL POWER!*

In 1838, I was granted a yearly income to continue my work from the British Association for the Advancement of Science and London's Geological Society. This really helped to pay the bills and was even more amazing considering the fact that as a female, I couldn't become a member.

Maria Pinney would often chide me that I was entirely too kind and too generous to my family. She would say to me, "Mary, you need to be smarter about money and take better care of yourself. It seems to me that whatever money you get by collecting fossils goes to your family or to anyone else that wants it."

And I am really happy to tell you that in 1839, my one and only paper about fossils was published in the *Magazine of Natural History.*

What do you think about that? I had no formal training, just a keen talent for fossils. For me, it was like getting a big stamp of approval from the science community that still did not allow women to be part of its membership ... well, not yet, anyway.

Maria Pinney wrote of me that my "learning had made me mad, and that I was afraid of no one." Oh Maria! MY LEARNING DID NOT MAKE ME MAD or CRAZY! I just didn't mind speaking up and having a different opinion, especially if I had a feeling that I knew EXACTLY what I was talking about. I could hold my own with any of the scientists who tried to question my finds or my science. Maybe one day a girl can speak her mind without everyone thinking she is not nice or off her rocker!

Louis Agassiz would later honor me and Elizabeth for helping him unlock the secrets of prehistoric fish. He even named a few species after me! I wonder how those fish fossils felt about being named after a GIRL?

# DIG THIS!

*In the 1840s, Agassiz named two fossil fish species after me —*
*Acrodus anningiae and Belenostomus anningiae.*

I also worked with Thomas Hawkin on his book *The Book of the Great Sea Dragons.* He was another great friend that gave me credit for helping him. He said, "Mary has given us all kinds of facts and ingenious theories." INGENIOUS? Ha ha! I'm an ingenious genius!

These fine men were the exception, and not the rule in my lifetime. In the same year Thomas and Louis made my name and work more known, Richard Owen wrote a paper on Plesiosaur macrocephalus and DID NOT MENTION ME AT ALL!

# DIG THIS!

*Richard Owen was a controversial biologist and paleontologist because his entire legacy is riddled with accusations of taking credit for other people's work.*

# SUPER DIG!

*Never take credit for something you didn't do!*
*Why would you even want to? Work hard, and make a name for yourself.*
*Never, ever, ever claim something as your own if it is not!*

I was diagnosed with breast cancer in 1845. When my friends at the Geological Society heard of my illness, they started a fund that paid for my treatment.

For the pain, I was given an opiate-based drug, laudanum, as a pain-killer. I refused to complain about my illness; so many folks in Lyme Regis mistook the effects of the drug for drunkenness. But I wasn't drunk; they just didn't know that I was battling cancer, a battle that I'm afraid I am losing.

## DIG THIS!

*In the minute books of the Geological Society,
the entry in July 1846 reads: "It is resolved that Miss Mary Anning be
requested to become an Honorary Member of the Institution."*

My time is growing short. With each passing day, I grow more and more sick. For all the miracles I've been granted in my life, I don't suppose I'll get another, except for maybe the will to keep on fossil hunting.

Sure, it's harder and harder for me to comb the beach for wonderful fossils, but I still go, even when I don't feel so great. I mean, you just never know when you might find something magnificent.

Holy FOSSILS! This just might just be the longest letter I have ever written! I'll close this letter remembering that I was truly one lucky lightning-struck girl! I didn't have lots of money, but I believe I was rich with fossils and knowledge.

Here at the end, I can say that I am very proud of the things I discovered, and I truly hope that I helped create a clearer picture of the history and the age of this world and all the creatures that once lived in it.

I won't get as much credit as I believe I deserved for all my finds, but that's not why I did what I did and why I went out daring to dig every day.

No one is better than I am at spotting a fossil; well, except for maybe my Daddy. I believe he would have been PROUD of me (and Joseph) for finding the creature he believed was lurking in the cliffs of Lyme Regis.

Remember this: if anyone ever tells you that you won't, can't, or shouldn't just because you're a a girl (or different or just who you are), you must prove them wrong, change their minds, AND that's how you'll change the world.

And now I invite you to write a letter to your genius self and imagine all that you will create, invent, and make known. Go ahead … I can't wait to see all that you will surely do! Remember, BE BRAVE, AND DARE TO DIG!

*Much Love* | MARY ANNING

# LETTER TO MY GENIUS SELF

_____

_____

_____

_____

_____

_____

_____

_____

_____

_____

# DIG THIS!

*So the next time you try to say, "She sells seashells by the seashore,"*
*think of me, a young girl pulling a fossilized,*
*prehistoric creature out of the sand!*

*P. S. If you ever find yourself in Lyme Regis,*
*please take a stroll on the beach and see what you can find.*

# Letter to Genius You
## Author's Note

Mary Anning died of breast cancer on March 9, 1847 and was buried at Lyme Regis Parish Church. Later her friends at the Geological Society eulogized her and paid for a stained-glass window to be installed in the church in her memory.

It depicts six charitable acts ... feeding the hungry, giving drink to the thirsty, clothing the naked, sheltering the homeless, visiting prisoners, and helping the sick.

The inscription reads: "This window is sacred to the memory of Mary Anning of this parish, who died 9 March AD 1847 and is erected by the vicar and some members of the Geological Society of London in commemoration of her usefulness in furthering the science of geology, as also of her benevolence of heart and integrity of life."

After her death, Mary's dear friend, Henry De la Beche, President of the Geological Society at that time, wrote a eulogy that he read to a meeting of the society and published in its quarterly transactions, WHICH WAS THE FIRST such eulogy given for a woman. This was an honor normally bestowed only on the male members of the society, which did not admit women until 1904.

The eulogy began: "I cannot close this notice of our losses by death without adverting to that of one, who though not placed among even the easier classes of society, but one who had to earn her daily bread by her labour, yet contributed by her talents and untiring researches in no small degree to our knowledge of the great Ichthyosaurs, and other forms of organic life entombed in the vicinity of Lyme Regis."

An uncredited author in the **All the Year Round** periodical, edited by Charles

Dickens, wrote of her in 1865 that "the carpenter's daughter has won a name for herself, and has deserved to win it."

And DIG THIS! In 2010, Mary Anning was named one of Britain's top ten most influential female scientists of all time… and she never even graduated high school or went to college! In fact, Mary Anning was called "the greatest fossilist the world ever knew" by the British Journal for the History of Science.

# OTHER BOOKS TO READ

*To learn more, read about Mary Anning, the fossil finding female with these books!*
*DARE TO DIG DEEP!*

*Stone Girl, Bone Girl: A Story of Mary Anning of Lyme Regis,* Laurence Aunoh

*Mary Anning, Fossil Hunter,* Anna Claybourne, Laura Totton

*Superheroes of Science: Mary Anning,* Robert Snedden

*Mary Anning, The Girl Who Cracked Open The World,* Debora Pearson

*History VIP: Mary Anning Fossil Hunter and Dinosaur Expert*
*(Brilliant Biographies of the Dead Famous),* Kay Barnham

*Jurassic Mary: Mary Anning and the Primeval Monsters,* Patricia Pierce

*Girls Who Looked Under Rocks: The Lives of Six Pioneering Naturalists,* Jeannine Atkins

*Rare Treasure: Mary Anning and Her Remarkable Discoveries,* Don Brown

*Mary Anning's Curiosity,* Monica Kulling

*The Fossil Girl,* Catherine Brighton

*The Official Guide to the Jurassic Coast,* Denys Brunsden

*DK Eyewitness: Rock and Fossil Hunter,* Ben Morgan

*Paleontology: The Study of Prehistoric Life,* Susan Heinrichs Gray

*Figuring Out Fossils,* Sally Walker

*Places to Visit*

Lyme Regis Museum, Bridge Street, Lyme Regis, Dorset
(https://www.lymeregismuseum.co.uk/"https://www.lymeregismuseum.co.uk/)

*Fun Websites to Visit*

http://jurassiccoast.org/fossilfinder/

http://kids.earth.nasa.gov/

https://ucmp.berkeley.edu/

http://paleoportal.org/

https://ucmp.berkeley.edu/fosrec/

https://ucmp.berkeley.edu/education/explotime.html/

https://epiccvfe.berkeley.edu/

http://www.nps.gov/subjects/fossils/fossil-parks.htm/

# GLOSSARY

*Ammonite* – an extinct, aquatic animal that was protected by a spiral-coiled shell made from calcium

*Anatomy* – the structure and features of an animal or plant

*Autodidact* – a person who has learned a subject without the benefit of a teacher or formal education; a self-taught person

*Belemnite* – the fossil of a prehistoric animal related to the squid and octopus

*Coprolites* – dung stones or fossilized poop

*Curiosities* – interesting or unusual items

*Dinosaur* – a reptile that roamed the earth millions of years ago (dinosaurs became extinct 65 million years ago)

*Dissenter* – someone who has or expresses an opinion different from a prevailing or official position; someone who disagrees with established beliefs

*Embedded* – fixed firmly and deeply in a surrounding solid mass

*Eulogy* – a speech in praise of someone who has died

*Evolution* – the gradual process in which something changes into a different and usually more complex or better form

*Extinction* – the disappearance of an animal from Earth over time

*Fossil* – the remains or traces of an animal, plant, or other organisms that over tens of thousands of years have been molded or turned into stone

*Fossilist* – a person who collects and studies fossils

*Genius* – extraordinary intellectual and creative power or a person of extraordinary intellect and talent

*Geologist* – an expert in the study of Earth

*Geology* – the science of rocks and the earth's history

*Grypahaea* – a genus of fossil shells related to the oyster that lived 66 to 140 million years ago

*Healing Salve* – a medicinal ointment that soothes and heals

*Ichthyosaur* – a large marine mammal; Ichthyosaur means 'fish lizard'

*Jurassic Age* – a prehistoric time period of 200-145 million years ago

*Jurassic Coast* – an area along the southern coast of England that is rich in fossils

*Limestone* – a common type of rock which often contains fossils

*Lithograph* – a print produced from a printing process in which the image to be printed is rendered on a flat surface, as on a sheet of zinc or aluminum, and treated to retain ink while the areas containing no images are treated to repel ink

*Mesozoic Era* – the geologic time between 250 and 65 million years ago;

*Meso* means *middle* and *zoic* is a word used in relation to animals. The Mesozoic Era was a huge era of diversified life forms and home to various species that marked the gap between older and primitive animals and modern complex animals, thus being the era of the 'middle animals.'

*Napoleon Bonaparte* – a French statesman and military leader who rose to prominence during the French Revolution and led several successful campaigns during the French Revolutionary Wars

*Napoleonic Wars* – wars which were fought during the rule of Napoleon Bonaparte over France. They started after the French Revolution ended and Napoleon Bonaparte became powerful in France in November 1799. War began between the United Kingdom and France in 1803.

*Overseers of the Poor* – in England, overseers of the poor administered poor relief such as money, food, and clothing as part of the Poor Law system. The position was created by the Act for the Relief of the Poor 1597.

*Paleontologist* – a scientist who studies fossils

*Paleontology* – the study of prehistoric life forms on earth through the examination of plant and animal fossils

*Plesiosaur* – a large marine mammal; *Plesiosaur* means *near lizard*

*Pterosaur* – flying reptile

*Pterodactyl* – a small flying reptile mammal; *Pterodactyl* means *winged finger*

*Remnant* – something left over; a remainder

*Scientist* – used for the first time in 1834 in William Whewell's review of Mary Somerville's book. It didn't seem right or appropriate to call her a *man* of science, so he coined the word to describe a woman of science; aka, *scientist.* So, truly, the word *scientist* originally described a woman in science

*Specimen* – an individual fossil, animal, rock, or other item used in scientific study or as an example

*Species* – a group of living things whose members are similar to each other.

*Time Capsule* – a sealed container preserving articles and records of contemporary culture for perusal by scientists and scholars of the distant future

*Tuberculosis* – an illness that affects the lungs, characterized by the coughing up of mucus and sputum, fever, weight loss, and chest pain

*Unsung* – not honored, acclaimed, or praised; uncelebrated

*Unconscious* – lacking awareness and the capacity for sensory perception; not conscious, temporarily lacking consciousness

*Upholster* –  putting the padded cushions and coverings on furniture such as sofas and armchairs

*Vertebrae* – the small bones that link together to form the backbone

*Vertebrate* – any animal having a backbone or spinal column; there are five classes of vertebrates: fish, amphibians, reptiles, birds, and mammals

# TIMELINE

5.21.1799: Born to Richard and Molly Anning, one of 10 children, only she and older brother Joseph survive.

8.19.1800: Mary Anning is struck by lightning … and survives.

11.1810: Richard Anning dies.

1811: Joseph finds ichthyosaur skull; Mary finds rest of skeleton. Lord Henry Hoste Henley pays family £23 for it and sells it to William Bullock.

1812: Henry De la Beche moves to Lyme Regis and befriends Mary and Joseph Anning; they become lifelong friends.

1814: Sir Everard Home writes a series of six papers on the Ichthyosaur describing it as a crocodile.

5.1819: Mary's Ichthyosaur skeleton is purchased at auction for £45/5s by Charles Konig of the British Museum. He gives the fossil its proper name.

5.15.1820: Thomas James Birch holds auction of Anning's fossils at Bullock's in London; raises £400 for the family. Mary finds Plesiosaur skeleton, undocumented.

1821: Letter from Molly Anning to British Museum requesting payment for a specimen; Henry de la Beche and William Conybeare collaborate on a paper describing Mary's Ichthyosaur. Mary finds Ichthyosaurus Platydon (now Temnodontosaurus platyodon) skeleton.

1823: Article in *The Bristol Mirror* credits her with nearly all specimens of Ichthyosaurs in great collections.

12.10.1823: Finds her first documented Plesiosaur.

1824: Lady Harriet Silvester in her diary records Anning's great knowledge. Conybeare presents Plesiosaur to Geological Society without crediting her find or sketches; Buckland presents Megalosaurus at same meeting. George Cuvier withdraws question of fraud in plesiosaur find. Anning suggests to Buckland that bezoars are fossilized feces.

1825: Joseph Anning leaves fossil business for upholstery business.

1826: Purchases home and store: Anning's Fossil Depot. Discovers ink sac in belemnite fossil.

1827: George William Featherstonehaugh purchases fossils from Anning for New York Lyceum of Natural History.

1828: Finds first British Pterosaur and Dapedium politum skeleton.

1829: Finds Squaloraja fish skeleton. Buckland credits her with Pterosaur find and with discovery of coprolites.

1830: Henry de la Beche paints *Duria Antiquior* and commissions George Scharf to make a lithograph for sale to support Anning. Anning leaves Congregationalist church for Anglican church. Anning finds nearly complete Plesiosaur skeleton.

12.1830: Finds new kind of Plesiosaur (Macrocephalus) and earns £200 for it.

10.1833: Landslide kills dog Tray and nearly kills Mary.

1834: Louis Agassiz visits Anning and hunts fossils with her and Elizabeth Philpot.

1835: Loses £300 in a bad investment, almost all of her life savings. William Buckland persuades British Association for the Advancement of Science to award her a civil list pension annuity of £25/year.

1839: Writes letter to the editor of *Magazine of Natural History* objecting to the classification of a fossilized shark; only writing published in her lifetime. Leads William Buckland, William Conybeare, and Richard Owen on a fossil hunting expedition.

1840: Richard Owen writes paper on Plesiosaur Macrocephalus; does not mention Anning. Sometime after this date, Louis Agassiz names two fish species after Anning: Acrodus anningiae and Belenostomus anningiae.

1844: King Frederick Augustus II of Saxony visits her shop and buys an Ichthyosaur skeleton; writes her name as Mary Annins. Mary tells the king's physician, "I am well known through all of Europe."

1846: Geological Society raises money to contribute to bills; Dorset County Museum names her a member.

3.9.1847: Dies of breast cancer.

1850: Geological Society dedicates a stained glass window in St. Michaels, a local church, to her memory.

1865: Is acclaimed in *All the Year Round* by Charles Dickens: "the carpenter's daughter has won a name for herself, and she has deserved to win it."

1904: Geological Society begins admitting women.

1908: Terry Sullivan writes "She Sells Seashells by the Seashore," said to be about Anning.

2010: Royal Society names Mary Anning as one of the top ten women in British history who had the most influence on science in celebration of the Society's 350th anniversary in 2010.

# OTHER SCIENTISTS

*Other Female Fossilists, Geologists, Archaelogists,
and Paleontologists you should read about:*

## MARY LEAKEY, FBA

This extraordinary fossil hunter and flint-point expert discovered several of our early ancestors, filling in blank spots on the tree of human evolution. The coolest thing she excavated? An 86-foot long trail of human footprints, dated at almost 4 million years ago, that proves our ancestors were already bipedal and had feet like ours that early in human history. "Basically, I have been compelled by curiosity. You only find what you are looking for." - Mary Leakey

## DR. CATHERINE BADGLEY, Paleoecologist
### *University of Michigan*

Badgley studies the ecology and geographic diversity patterns of mammals in relation to changing environmental gradients. She and her students document the paleo-environments of regions with rich mammalian fossil assemblages and analyze changes in diversity and ecological attributes of mammals over time and across landscapes.

## DR. ANDREA HAWKES, Micropaleontologist
*University of North Carolina, Wilmington*

Hawkes reconstructs the frequency and magnitude of coastal hazards (tsunamis, earthquakes, hurricanes, sea level) using fossil single-celled marine organisms (foraminifera) found in salt marsh sediments up to 10,000 years old.

## PROF. CAROLE S. HICKMAN, Invertebrate Paleontologist
*University of California, Berkeley*

Hickman has devoted more than 50 years to field and laboratory investigations of fossil and living marine mollusks in an effort to develop general principles of animal architecture and evolution.

## DR. KAY BEHRENSMEYER, Vertebrate Paleontologist
*Smithsonian Institution*

Behrensmeyer investigates how vertebrate remains become fossilized and what fossils tell us about ancient ecology. She studies processes that preserve and destroy modern bones in East Africa and uses this information to help her decipher stories told by fossil bones.

DR. PENNY HIGGINS, Vertebrate Paleontologist and Geochemist
*University of Rochester*

Higgins uses the chemistry of fossils - specifically stable isotopes of carbon and oxygen from fossilized teeth, shells, and other fossilized skeletal materials to examine weather and climate patterns of the remote past.

DR. SARA B. PRUSS, Paleontologist
*Smith College*

Pruss studies ancient interactions between animals and their environment during evolutionary events and mass extinctions. In her work, she pursues questions like: "Why did organisms first make shells?" and "What happened to Earth when 90% of the animals died?"

# About the Author

Janet Ivey-Duensing, Emmy award-winning children's media creator, host of Janet's Planet, Inc., and current President of Explore Mars, Inc. is author of *Daring to Dig, Mary Anning: Fossil Hunter* which is the first book in a planned series called "Unsung Genius" which celebrates scientists (especially women and other minorities) and highlights their genius.

Janet narrates the story of renowned nineteenth-century paleontologist Mary Anning in the first person as Mary writing a letter to her younger self (and to the GENIUS in the young reader) to remember and celebrate her accomplishments throughout her lifetime. In this way, Janet gives women (who did not have a voice in the time and era in which they lived) the opportunity to speak and tell their own story. The result is as historic and factual an account possible of Mary's great discoveries, her friendships with notable scientists of the day, and her love of exploration and all things fossil. At the end of the book, Mary invites the reader to write "A Letter To Your Genius Self," where the reader can create a vision of what genius they want to bring forth in their lifetime.

Janet is an advocate, educator, communicator, and female role model of STEM/STEAM and is committed to sharing the joy of exploration and discovery with children around the globe. Janet's mission is to encourage science literacy globally and particularly to embody female science mentors for the next generation of women in space and science.

Janet lives by a lake outside Nashville with her husband and her two puppies, Dude and Bunny. She has four grandchildren who call her Jan-Jan.

*You can find Janet at the following places:*

www.janetsplanet.com
Facebook: Janet's Planet
Twitter: JanetsPlanet
YouTube: JanetsPlanetOfficial
Instagram: JanetsPlanetOfficial
Email: janet@janetsplanet.com

# About the Illustrator

Katie Grayson is an artist and illustrator from Nashville, Tennessee. The oldest of six children, she learned early to escape into her imagination, where she fell in love with dinosaurs, astronauts, sharks, and dragons. After studying art seriously for the past eight years, she is launching a career in commercial art with murals, logos, and artwork for books. She is also working on writing and illustrating a series of children's books that celebrate kids from diverse backgrounds in fantasy and science fiction environments.

## MEET EVIE!

# MARY ANNING ROCKS!

Some people might be wondering, who is Mary Anning? Well don't worry, you are not alone. Most of the time when I ask anyone about her, they don't know who she is, and they don't know what I'm talking about.

My name is Evie Swire. I am eleven years old and live in a small village in Dorset near the sea, along the Jurassic Coast. When I was eight years old, we learnt all about Mary in my school class. We did a whole project, and I thought because I did it at school everyone in the whole world would be learning about her, too. Then I found out that they weren't, and it made me feel like I had to do something about it

My mummy also said that schools were very good at teaching about the amazing things men have discovered and invented, like Issac Newton, Albert Einstein, and Charles Darwin, but not so good at talking about women in history and what they have discovered and done. If it wasn't for Mary's discoveries of fossilised creatures, Charles Darwin would probably have not been able to start his own discoveries; so she is very important, and that's why I want to build her a statue.

If you want know more about my campaign Mary Anning Rocks and want to help me build Mary her statue, go to my website www.maryanningrocks.co.uk

CPSIA information can be obtained
at www.ICGtesting.com
Printed in the USA
BVHW091010080720
583180BV00007B/105